I'M GOING TO CALIFORNIA
YO VOY A CALIFORNIA

"See you in the movies!"
Mary Wade

Featuring

Author
Mary Dodson Wade

Illustrator
Virginia Marsh Roeder

Conlea Roeder
you can be a star!

Translator
Juan M. Aguayo

COLOPHON HOUSE ⊤⊤ HOUSTON, TEXAS

For a clutch of California cousins,
with special memories of
Elizabeth,
and for those two California cohorts, Steph and Judy
---M.D.W.

For Pratt, Andrew, and Emily
---V.M.R.

For my wonderful parents, Aida and Juan.
---J.M.A.

Cataloging-in-Publication Data
Wade, Mary Dodson
  I'm going to California/Yo voy a California/by Mary Dodson Wade;
trans. by Juan M. Aguayo; illus. by Virginia Marsh Roeder.
  p. cm.
Summary: California fun beckons everyone.
ISBN 1-882539-21-4
ISBN 1-882539-22-2 (pbk)
[1. California—Fiction. 2. California—Description and Travel. 3. Spanish
language materials—Bilingual. 4. Stories in rhyme.] I. Roeder, Virginia Marsh, ill.
II. Aguayo, Juan M., tr. III. Title
PZ7W12IC 1997
917.94
[E]

"I'm going to California.
I'll be a movie star."

*Yo voy a California.
Seré estrella de cine.*

"There are stars over Hollywood
but millions more at Palomar."

*Hay estrellas sobre Hollywood,
pero millones más en Palomar.*

"I'll drive a car without a top and live in a great big house."

Manejaré un auto sin capota y viviré en una casa grande.

"You can ride cable cars or dance with a mouse."

Puedes pasear en tranvías o bailar con un ratón.

"I'll wear sparkly dresses and turn letters on a show."

*Me vestiré con trajes brillantes y voltearé letras
en un espectáculo.*

"In March we'll watch swallows come back to Capistrano."

En marzo veremos las golondrinas regresar a Capistrano.

"I'll be the beautiful lady in the gorilla's hand."

Seré la dama hermosa en la mano del gorila.

"There are zoos for animals,
but mammoths once walked the land."

*Hay zoológicos para animales,
pero los mamuts caminaron antes por la tierra.*

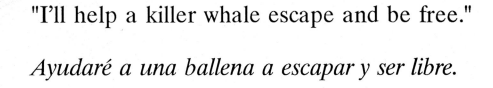

"I'll help a killer whale escape and be free."

Ayudaré a una ballena a escapar y ser libre.

"Whales glide down the coast, and seals sun by the sea."

Las ballenas se deslizan por la costa, y las focas se solean en el mar.

"I'll be a vampire and make people shiver."

Seré un vampiro y a la gente haré temblar.

"Some say they've seen Big Foot.
Others found gold in the river."

*Algunos dicen que vieron un Big Foot.
Otros encontraron oro en el río.*

"I'll leap tall buildings or swing from a vine."

Saltaré edificios altos o me meseré en una liana.

"We'll walk through redwoods and sing in the sunshine."

*Caminaremos a través de redwoods gigantes
y cantaremos bajo el sol.*

"I can look like Elvis or be a cowboy on a horse."

Puedo parecerme a Elvis, o ser un vaquero en un caballo.

"It's possible in California to be anything, of course."

Es posible en California ser cualquier cosa, por supuesto.

"They'll put a star in the sidewalk.
It will say my name."

Me pondrán una estrella en la acera.
Llevará mi nombre.

"California is great fun.
You'll love it just the same!"

California es una gran diversión.
¡De seguro te gustará!

CRUISING CALIFORNIA

Northern California

Enjoy Paul Bunyan Days in Fort Bragg on Labor Day weekend.

Take the Skunk Train, an old logging train, from Fort Bragg to Willits.

Enter the Redwood National Park at Orick and find redwoods as tall as a 36-story building.

Hold your nose as you watch bubbling mud pots belch sulfur smells in Lassen Volcanic National Park.

Stand on the bluffs at Patrick's Point State Park to watch migrating gray whales or playful sea lions.

Observe huge trout from a bridge over the Truckee River outlet to Lake Tahoe in Tahoe City.

See Native American whalebone masks and seal-intestine parkas at End of the Trail Museum in Klamath.

San Francisco Bay Area

Ride San Francisco's cable cars, visit Chinatown, explore sailing ships and the aquarium at Fisherman's Wharf, unlock the mysteries of science at the Exploratorium.

Take the boat to Alcatraz and see how prisoners once lived.

Cross the Golden Gate Bridge to Muir Woods National Monument to see giant redwoods.

Watch birds and whales at Point Reyes National Seashore and walk down 300 steps to the lighthouse.

Operate robots at the Tech Museum of Innovation in San Jose.

At Santa Cruz, enjoy the 1924 Big Dipper roller coaster.

Watch elephant seals at Año Nuevo State Reserve.

Join San Francisco's Chinese New Year Festival in February and the Cherry Festival in April.

Central California Coast

Gaze at Morro Rock, a 576-foot-tall volcanic dome in Morro Bay, where peregrine falcons nest.

Wander through the 100 rooms of the Hearst Castle near San Simeon.

Enjoy the beauty of the Big Sur area.

Explore rugged Point Lobos State Reserve, an ocean preserve featuring sea mammals.

View an indoor sea behind a huge window at the Monterey Bay Aquarium.

In the spring, join the Hans Christian Andersen Fairy Tale Festival in Solvang.

Participate in Old Spanish Days' Children's Parade in August in Santa Barbara.

Los Angeles Area

Observe the La Brae Tar Pits and find remains of mammoths and saber-tooth tigers in the Page Museum.

At Griffith Park, enjoy the Gene Autry Western Heritage Museum, the observatory, and a merry-go-round.

Watch the Blessing of the Animals procession on Olvera Street on the day before Easter.

Go behind the scenes of movies at Warner Bros. in Burbank and take in Universal Studios Hollywood.

Watch Pasadena's Rose Bowl Parade on New Year's Day.

Marvel at the half-million Native American artifacts at the Southwest Museum.

Tour the luxury liner *Queen Mary*, docked at Long Beach.

Take off for Catalina Island to ride glass-bottom boats or a semi-submersible submarine, or try snorkeling.

Discover Disneyland in Anaheim and Knott's Berry Farm in Buena Park.

In San Juan Capistrano, watch swallows return to the mission in March.

Join the Butterfly Parade to welcome Monarchs back to Pacific Grove in October.

Find the incredible Watts Towers.

Enjoy music, theater and entertainment at Orange County's Imagination Celebration in late spring.

Lower California Coast

Imagine life in early California at a restored adobe in Old Town San Diego State Historic Park.

At San Diego's Balboa Park, watch an underwater hippo ballet and visit history and art museums. Native Americans share their stories and art at the Museum of Man in June.

In downtown San Diego, visit the *Star of India* windjammer. Take the ferry or drive over the bridge to Coronado Island. Shamu is at Sea World in Mission Bay, San Diego.

Observe African and Asian animals at the San Diego Wild Animal Park in Escondido.

In La Jolla, visit the Scripps Institution of Oceanography or watch California gray whales in winter. Find surprises at the Mingei International Museum of World Folk Art.

At Mount Palomar, view the Hale Telescope, the second-largest one in the world.

Tour the Arco Olympic Training Center in Chula Vista.

Enjoy the Mother Goose Parade in El Cajon around Thanksgiving.

Interior Valleys, Mountains, and Deserts

Visit Hanford's China Alley to see how early railroad workers lived.

Find restored locomotives at the California State Railroad Museum in Sacramento.

Walk the banks of the river and view miners' equipment in Marshall Gold Discovery State Historic Park.

Pan for gold in Jamestown, or visit the world's largest gem and mineral collection at the California State Mining and Mineral Museum in Mariposa.

Enter the Calaveras County Fair Jumping Frog Jubilee contest at Angels Camp in May.

At Indian Grinding Rock State Historic Park, observe over 1000 cup-like places made by the Miwok tribe.

Visit the ghost town of "Big, Bad Bodie."

Marvel at Yosemite Falls and Half Dome, a granite peak overlooking the valley in Yosemite National Park.

Gaze at huge, neatly-formed basalt columns in the Devil's Postpile National Monument.

Find twisted bristlecone pines that are more than 4,700 years old in Inyo National Forest east of Bishop.

Walk more than 100-feet just to circle one redwood tree in Sequoia and Kings Canyon National Parks.

Watch whimsically-painted oil well pumps bob up and down at the "Iron Zoo" just north of Coalinga.

Visit Santa's Village at Big Bear Lake.

Interact with exhibits at A Special Place children's museum in San Bernadino.

Pick your own apples at Yucaipa and Cherry Valley or visit the California Citrus State Historical Park in Riverside.

See cowboy movie mementoes at the Roy Rogers/Dale Evans Museum in Victorville.

Near Blythe, marvel at intaglios, giant figures scraped into the earth by prehistoric inhabitants.

See volcanic cinder cones at Mojave National Preserve.

Visit the Calico Early Man site near Barstow.

Perhaps you can see a shuttle land at Edwards Air Force Base.

Explore sand dunes, borax mines, many-colored formations, and even spring cactus blossoms in Death Valley.

Observe petroglyphs at Petroglyph Canyon near Ridgecrest.

Don't miss the chain of missions founded by Father Junipero Serra along the coast, the snow-capped peaks of Mount Shasta and Mount Whitney, the groves of fruit and vegetables in the valleys, or the poppies and lupines on the hillsides.

Text set in 18 pt. Tymes Roman type
display in 32 pt. Arrus Block
Printed on 80# Mead Moistrite Matte paper
Mixed media art
Printing and binding by Walsworth

Author Mary Dodson Wade loves to travel, and California's variety of scenery and history makes it a favorite place to visit. A former librarian, she usually writes nonfiction, but this book allows her to combine the best of both fiction and nonfiction worlds.

Illustrator Virginia Marsh Roeder, with training in graphic design at Pratt Institute in New York, worked as a successful commercial illustrator before moving to Houston, Texas, where she taught art. Her latest career is in illustrating children's books.

Translator Juan M. Aguayo, born in Puerto Rico, came to the United States as an Army officer in 1986. He holds a Master's Degree in Mass Communications and Speech, has taught courses at the university level, and is a former public information specialist for the Houston Department of Health and Human Services.